AF295416

Josefin Winther

To Vega

Photo: Per Heimly
Translator: Hege Jakobsen Lepri

Publisher: BoD – Books on Demand, Oslo, Norge
Print: BoD – Books on Demand, Norderstedt, Tyskland

ISBN: 978-82-845-1096-5

INTRODUCTION

Dear reader,

This is my story. It's been written step by step as I walked on my life's journey. What is expressed here, are my reflections, based on how the world appeared to me in that moment—right there. I hope you will feel the constant motion that has been part of the experience. I hope you feel the transformation. Hedvig and Vega are the two people that are closest to me. They have their own versions of this story, their own journeys.

In this text, Hedvig, the person who is with me—is often referred to as "she." The title of this book is, "To Vega." This title has a double meaning. The deep connection I feel with Vega has been with me a long time. But this story is more than anything about my path to Vega.

I want to thank Hedvig for all that she's given me—above all, a daughter. She gave me her blessing to share this story. I have also created music alongside the writing process. This music was released simultaneously with the book—as an EP titled "Til Vega."

Thank you, Vega, that you were willing to come here—to us.

If you really want to know an author, look for what they don't write about

BE WELCOME!

Less than an hour after you had been transferred, we started a fight. We were both off keel because something that should have been a festive occasion, felt more like a clinical assembly line. We spent 15 minutes in total inside the clinic, before we once again were ejected into the street—now bewildered by the idea we might be pregnant. Each of us had her own way of dealing with this, and we launched into a mindless quarrel. There was all that adrenalin rushing through my body, and I lost the handle of myself. Again.

Of course you had no wish to come into something like that. Only a short hour after the transfer into my body, a tidal wave of wickedness came washing over you. Anyone would have turned on their heel at the entrance if they saw something like that.

But you weren't there. You never were. So, the quarrel was of no consequence. But it felt like I had scared you away. Again.

DECISION

I was rambling around the forest by our house. A full year of failed attempts had passed, and today another one was over. I was losing my footing and started to feel desperate for something—anything—to hold on to. I realized what I had to do was write. I had to write about what I never wanted to write about. I had to write about you.

YOU WHO CAN SEE EVERYTHING

We have this habit of saying "She'll come when she's supposed to come. All things are as they are supposed to be." And in one way, this brings us comfort. In another way, it makes everything meaningless. Why should I wait, when you know it all? Why should I hope, when your path isn't bound by this hope? If there's a meaning behind everything, it all becomes a practice of letting things happen. Later, I will learn what I was supposed to learn.

Because you know what you're supposed to do. You have always held that knowledge. A person who can see through your eyes, sees everything. You knew you weren't supposed to come. You may never come. There's a chance, "you" do not exist. But I have felt a closeness to you since I learned your name. Vega. Wild and wonderful. Dark and warm.

I have crafted an image of you, subconsciously. There's a resemblance with me, but you're calmer. You are like me, but without all the scars, the ego and all that spiritual flotsam.

But why should you resemble me? I feel lonely on this earth, I beg you to come to me. If you're here to comfort me—or even save me, it would be better if you weren't like me. But all acts of creation are about creating something in your own image. Even creating a human being. Some evenings I walk on the path by our house just to listen to you in the wind. The wind brushes through the leafy tree crowns, producing a low breathing sound. I look up and meet the gaze of the stars. And suddenly, you're there. I stretch my arms up, and say "Come to me! Please, just come to me now!"

There are times when I daydream about just allowing myself to lie down on the forest floor, below ferns and heath. To be at peace. To be at peace with critters and creepy things that would soon find me. To be at peace with the disintegration. To feel pleasure at being dissolved so that I can return home to you.

TIME IS A HILL PLAYING WITH EVERY WOUND

A year ago, the pain was pure. Almost virginal. An innocent pain, without any shadows. How well I remember the first time you didn't arrive.

Mid-summer. I was on a train from Bergen to Oslo. And my period arrived. I cried and felt the pain building in me. It was such an innocent pain; it almost dissipated the same moment it appeared. Nothing lumpy, no rot, no story. It was only painful to know you wouldn't arrive. And I kept going in faith. *Next time.*

In the resting room after the sixth attempt, I rest with my head in her lap. And right then, there's an epiphany that you are there, alive inside me. At least for a few minutes. Both of us cry, and the knowledge you may decide to die at any moment in there, is hard. But it is marvelous to think that at any moment you may decide to live. This may be the closest I'll ever come to being pregnant.

This is the sixth time you didn't arrive, and the pain has morphed into different shapes. This time I knew before I knew, because I dreaded the pain. I took in the disappointment and self-loathing in advance. Not least, I dreaded getting my period. The loathsome message "just forget about it. This is us, peeling off the lining from the uterine wall. Nothing inside here could survive now."

During the night, I felt the menstrual pain sneaking up on me. A bodily premonition. I tried to tell myself I was imagining it all. Or maybe this is what it felt like to be pregnant. I've had that naive thought a few times now: "Is this something you feel if you're pregnant perhaps?"

Today I had my blood tests and was informed over the phone that the value was twenty-five something or other—which is a negative number. My period hasn't arrived yet, but the pain is building.

21.05.2022

WHO NEEDS STATS WHEN THERE'S KARMA?

A year ago, emotions like doubt and self-loathing were foreign to me. If I had read any of the many self-help books, I would have known this was coming. But is there really any help in knowing things in advance? I lived in a state of ignorant bliss back then. Your delivery is timed down to the minute. And everything has been done as correctly as possible to help you come to us. Someone at the clinic quotes statistics to comfort me, but I cannot stop thinking about my five siblings who all have had children. How often do they actually have sex?

But who would choose to come to this earth and be a result of work in a lab? Who would choose to spend their first five days in a small container, only to be frozen for an indefinite time? Who wants to have a father who is just a "straw"—purchased on a kind of dating app for sperm? Have I become one of these women in their late thirties, desperate for a baby? Have I been come intoxicated by the western fixation on self-realization, where a child suddenly is the only solution? Have I turned into some materialistic cowboy who stops at nothing to obtain what I think I want?

I buy a child from an industry where the gynecologist who comforts me one moment, tells me right after, there's a rebate if I buy bundles of three. After my appointment, they send me a text where they tell me I can pay you off in installments. I understand all the doubts you have, Vega. I would have the same doubts. It is quite a peculiar destiny to choose for oneself.

SHE WHO WAITS FOR SOMETHING GOOD ...

How does a person wait? Hope may turn into a demand. Faith may turn into superstition. Trust may turn into resignation. Longing may turn into obsession.

I have waited sincerely, touched my belly regularly. I have thought "now that you're there, I will try to slow down. You and I, Vega."

I have treasured the idea that you may have arrived. In the aftermath it hurts to have waited in this way. Because it only means I may have been walking around for ten days without being pregnant, an touched my own belly like a crazy person. One of those who push a doll around in a stroller and believe it is alive.

In the beginning, I was full of optimism. I thought, I have a healthy body, I have a playful disposition, I have an inspired mind. I thought someone like me would have to be a fertile woman. I knew my mother was fertile. My dad called her the primordial woman. They had six children. I inherited my mom's thick, dark hair. I thought, someone with such thick, dark hair, who tans so well in the summer, someone with such an appetite, who loves children as loudly as I do, such a person would have to be fertile. I practiced thinking I was.

Bit by bit I've come to understand I am not particularly young, and evidently not very fertile. Soon I will be a little bit old, and I feel stupid to have thought all those wonderful things about myself. I didn't mean to be arrogant, but I guess I was. I think about all the years I let pass. The years when I was young, when I could have had you on my first attempt. When you could have had a grandmother—rather than a mother—in her fifties to celebrate your confirmation. Fifteen neglected years. But back then, having a child was unthinkable for me. Despite wanting to become a mother. Or rather, I thought I would become a father.

And if I tried to think about being pregnant, I found it repulsive, like being violated. I was caught between the desire to have a child—and a desire to not be a woman. I tried to imagine ways I could carry a child in me, and thought that for that to happen, I would have to spend my pregnancy on a deserted island. Nobody could see me like that.

FINDING JOSEFIN, THE WOMAN

What made me hate my femininity? Sometimes I believe something happened in a prior lifetime. That my aversion against men is existential. That I was subjected to terrible things—wounds it will take several lifetimes to heal from. Maybe women carry collective trauma due to all that has been inflicted on us throughout history. The mere idea of opening my legs, whatever the context, makes me jumpy, makes me want to protect myself.

I became a tomboy when I was quite young. It was the only way I dared behave. Slowly I started losing touch with what I had in me that could make me a woman. I learned to hide anything that could hint at femininity, both to myself and others. During my teen years, I went through fire and water to hide that I was on my period. I couldn't reveal myself. If anyone saw through my cover and discovered I was a woman (which everyone knew I was), they wouldn't like me. Whoever may feel attracted to me, would no longer be attracted to me. Those who were my friends, wouldn't approve of the concept. I had to be super-human, with an athlete's physique, the behaviour of a well-versed man in his late twenties. And I had to have the sensitivity, humour and awareness of a girl of 19. I managed to coach my sweethearts and friends to participate in this game, and after a while they went beyond accepting it and became my accomplices in creating me as some kind of… man. Sometimes they wanted it more than I wanted it myself. It hurt. And I hated men. I hated men because they were something I couldn't become. And I hated men because they were something I didn't want to have.

When I turned thirty-five, bit by bit my world had been turned on its head. I was loved, not despite, but because of my femininity. At first, I didn't believe her. I thought she was making fun of me. But slowly I started to understand she loved me for who I was. And there is still a corner of me that cannot fully believe it. At first, when she talked about my feminine sides and my womanly body, it made me shudder. I mean, literally shiver. But slowly but surely even my body started believing it may be true. That it may be a good thing for me to be a woman. I had long known I didn't want to be a man, but never before had I felt this desire to be a woman. I discovered a force that I hadn't tapped into before. A force from deep within myself. And then one day, carrying a child in my body, no longer felt unthinkable. And then it became the only thing I wanted.

YOU CAN GET GOOD AT A WIDE VARIETY OF THINGS

At first, I was terrified of climbing into the gynecologist's chair. This fear grew after that first time when I had been examined in a very painful way. There was a balloon that had to be inflated inside my uterus. A liquid had to be squirted inside. Just thinking about it makes me feel bad. I cried out loudly and wept from the pain. I hope nobody in the waiting room were nervous about their appointment.

At this point I've climbed into the gynecologist's chair to be inseminated, to do ultrasounds, to perform a transfer, close to fifteen times. I can leave my job for 20 minutes—and in the meantime zip to the clinic, open my legs, watch the monitor, follow the measurement of the thickness of the mucosa and the area of the follicle—and then zip back.

"17 mm, ok. Then things are working according to plan, that should indicate transfer in the middle of next week. The ovulation injection tomorrow night and Cyclogest from Friday. Not a problem." I've become good at this. It gives me a feeling I'm coping well. We humans are adaptable.

I have also been through retrieval of eggs following hormone treatment. That's when I learned to inject myself since it had to be done several times a day for ten days. The extraction in itself was brutal. I had been given strong pain killers to take an hour before I came to the clinic. At that point, I was all by myself on a train.

It turned into a tragicomedy where I tottered like a drunk person off the train and struggled my way up the stairs to the clinic. I was slurring my speech when I presented myself at the reception. This was the state I had been in out among the people I usually commute together with to work. The retrieval was performed, and the pain was as bad as the time with the balloon examination. I could feel the small pinches inside the uterus, I observed as the eggs were picked up — one by one. Afterwards, I sat in the resting room weeping from the pain.

They gave me more pain killers. And then I was once again at the station, tottering into a train. That night, I fell asleep seated, in the middle of a family visit with an aunt I hadn't seen in a long time.

The results from the retrieval were excellent. Seven good eggs were fertilized and frozen. They had retrieved even more, but these were the good ones. Finally, a high note, after half a year of lows following my natural cycle. My mom called them "the seven sisters." Imagine if we were to have seven children! One more than in my own group of siblings.

But the seven sisters don't exist anymore. There are four left now, and maybe none of them are you.

ARE WE THERE YET?

"How much are you willing to sacrifice?" a friend asked as she examined me with her gaze. I didn't have an answer to give her. I felt I looked stupid seen through her eyes. The question has returned to me since. "How much are you willing to sacrifice? How far are you willing to go?" There is an inner voice asking this question, sometimes it's hers, sometimes it's mine. I cannot answer. The premise of the question is wrong, because it assumes this is an assessment I make. As if I continually ponder if I should spend 40,000 more, if I should try one more time, if I should stick it out for another month, if I should cry another tear. But there's not as much as a hint of an assessment happening. If I were telling the truth, I would take a deep look into my friend's eyes and tell her: "I am willing to sacrifice everything."

It feels strange to be willing to do anything for something that doesn't exist. But I cannot imagine my life continuing without you. To me, you already exist, so moving on would mean leaving you behind.

AS IT IS IN HEAVEN

Lately, I've been feeling ashamed of who I am. Nobody knows. Just me. And you, of course. I do understand you don't want to come to me. I understand it well. I try as hard as I can to improve. But I notice my thoughts turn dark and that I've entered a dark path—I try to envision myself as a human being. Envision a space where heaven and hell are separate. A vast space that is made from only a human being on this earth. But I feel like a wretched human. I don't like seeing it written, because I don't identify as someone who doesn't love herself. I have always been proud to be someone who appreciates who they are, but something has started wearing down that conviction. My thought patterns and emotions are no longer under my control. Such dark, putrid emotions. I feel like a small bark boat, like the ones I made as a child, adrift on the wide-open sea. There are times when the weather is fair and calm, and I believe I'm a decent, good person. Then a storm comes on, and I become who I really am. A tiny piece of bark—with a hole in the middle where the trusting hand of a child has inserted a small stick. I cannot sail. I cannot steer the vessel. I am merely drifting around.

Sometimes I find it unfair that I am judged by someone who is still with God. You too will find it difficult to be a human. It's no small feat to take on an earthly form. You too will have uncomfortable feelings— you too will feel disappointment. You will hurt people, lie and gorge yourself. You too will develop your patterns, your indolence, think your own thoughts. You will become the earthly embodiment of yourself. Nobody knows me as well as you do. It's not easy to make a good impression on someone who sees all. That's why I try from time to time to think that since you can see everything, you can also see I'm a good person, in spite of my shortcomings. If you can see everything, you must see I am doing the best I can. For they who see everything, surely do not judge.

THE SONG OF THE RED RUBY

In the end, Ask Burlefot understands what love is all about. That we humans, deep down, are alone in this world. "Love is something others don't know about. Love is a lonely thing," he says.

I dream about you making this life less lonely for me. I carry this fantasy that parents have a more profound experience of love, which makes their loneliness less persistent. I believe that the loneliness may remain, but you would provide it with some direction.

23.05.2022

TO ERR IS HUMAN, TO FORGIVE DIVINE

It's been three days since you didn't arrive, and I am once again flabbergasted by how life continues. The raw, dark pain is faded and subdued. Becoming more like a memory. Time plays tricks on me while I wait. And imagine, to you, time doesn't exist. All is being. Some of my hope feels more prominent than it was, as if going through this pain may make hope grow. I'm filled with mercy. I forgive myself for being who I am. I wrote that you judge me, but you, of course, do not judge anyone. I didn't mean to say that. I just got lost in self-pity. You don't judge, you just are, and see and love all. I hope you can carry some of the love to this earth and light up every room you enter.

TOWARDS VEGA

I am on a flight from Bergen, where I should have been at work. On my way to my fourth transfer, firmly convinced I'll focus on inner peace. I've tried to plan and live my life for a year based on the premise "your cycle determines everything." There's a huge contrast with the otherwise structured life I lead, now that my uterus—interacting mysteriously with the moon—decides the agenda.

We met in the lobby, and they asked us to sign the usual form. It was full of our signatures from earlier attempts. I signed and evaded the gaze of the receptionist. We entered the waiting area, and immediately, the tears started flowing. The doctor asked if I needed a few minutes, but what good would a few extra minutes do? Wasn't I waiting for you?

The transfer went well. It was performed while I was still weeping. Not from the pain but from exhaustion. I didn't dare get my hopes up. I didn't have the strength to stay upright for you.

TWO LINES UNDER THE ANSWER

We wanted to be together when we found out, so we did a home pregnancy test before the blood tests. I was prepared for it to be negative. I put down the test, glanced at my watch. 10:43. At 10:48 we would be able to go back into the bathroom to see. I heard a voice inside me saying "God has a plan for each one of us." What a sudden traditional twist to my religion! OK, I was religious, but this was one step away from going full Catholic. I ventured down the stairs and was fully ready to accept the negative result. We entered the bathroom together—and there it was, with its two lines. Two very clear plum-red lines. We jumped. "What? Is it positive?" Now, as this was our reality, the coffee we had on the stairs touched by the morning sun, became a festive occasion I will never forget. We had an inner smile. Our little smile.

20.06.2022

I WAS LONGING

Who did I long for? Me or you? Where do I end
in this longing, where do you begin?
My whole life you have longed for me
Years and days of faith and toil just to be
My whole life you have looked for me
Joined hands in prayer, taken steps to see
I was longing, I was your creed
I was hope, your blood from my seed
I was the eyes, I was the hands
I was the feet that carried your plans
Your whole life, you've been singing my song
Been in reverence, returned before long
All through the night, you waited for dawn
The light waned—hope became drawn

I was the tone, I was the defeat
I was the night, I was hate—so deep
I was the time you hurried through
I was the shadow thrown by you
I was never. You were always. Me.
I was tears
I was loss
I am hope

22.06.2022

STUDIO 54

There was an unanswered phone-call from the clinic after the blood test. There was no need to hurry and call them back. We were indeed pregnant. It could wait. Then we got on the line, and they told us the hCG value was 54. But that is much better than 25, I thought innocently. It turned out 25 was the absolute minimum to be considered a pregnancy. Maybe I only had a low baseline, and then everything was OK. But it may also be the case that this was a chemical pregnancy. I had never heard about such a thing. What happens is, your body believes it's got pregnant and starts producing the right hormone. There had to be a follow-up blood test, one that showed the number had grown, if not, it would be all over. My mom was so sad when I told her. We were visiting my brother when I shared the ambiguous news. I was pregnant, but… I explained about hCG values and growth curves.

I was suddenly able to lecture on this subject too. Throughout the day, I had checked the blood test app several times an hour. Every time the glimmering hope to see a higher number than 54. Evening fell, and it became time to go home. My sister-in-law urged me to check the results one last time. I told her that there certainly wouldn't be anyone sitting there analyzing blood tests at eleven o clock at night, but I couldn't convince her.

While brushing my teeth, I logged on and the number appeared: 195. The number shone back like the win in a lottery drawing. I ran into my mom's. We cried with joy and embraced each other.

28.06.2022

FIX ÁNEY

We're on vacation. I have been on many vacations in my life, often together with my large flock of siblings and their children. But this is the first time I feel we are all there. She, I—and now you too. We hop from one island to the next in the Aegean Sea. The wind plays with our hair, and we embrace each other frequently in implicit bliss. We have fun with ordering non-alcoholic beer for me. "How about this one, how bad do you think it is? That one was actually pretty good, only a hint of dishwashing detergent." We laugh. We relish all that hints that you're on your way.

PAIN IS INEVITABLE. SUFFERING IS A CHOICE.

Vega. And there I thought our story would be over now. I thought there would be nothing more to say, except a chapter about us living happily ever after. Didn't we have those two lines under our answer?! Despite the slow start for the hCG, 195 was a huge leap forward. There was no longer any doubt then. Something real was happening. I was pregnant for certain. Since then, we have been enjoying the thought that you exist for real. Not just in heaven anymore—now also on earth. Every time I've gone to the bathroom since the day with the two lines, my pulse has increased every time I've wiped myself. Fear of blood. It's has dissipated and was almost gone, but yesterday it was suddenly back. The bastard! There wasn't a lot of blood, but there was blood. You are a little more than four weeks old. We googled and found that this was rather common, as long as it wasn't accompanied by pain. Two pregnancy tests confirmed you were still there. Today there was more blood, and the accompanying pain was stronger. We went back to the pharmacy a little while ago. The same lady as yesterday served us. I heard myself ask "May I have a pregnancy test?" inside the pharmacy—in the cliché of clichés of sunny vacations, Platanias in Chania. It's our second day in a row, and the woman at the cash register tried to meet my shifty eyes. Life has a sense of humour.

We've practiced keeping calm. For almost two days we tried to let everything be as it was, all while it ached a little bit too far down in my belly for it to be a bellyache. Then finally it burst. The uterus contracted the way it has done every month for the past 23 years. It is a feeling I know through and through. I negotiate deeply with my womb. «No!

Don't do it. You're making the place unlivable for Vega if you start contracting now. She cannot sustain it. She is only 1.5 millimeters large, and she's working on attaching herself to your wall. Please, she can't take any more cramps now!"

I feel a lot going on in there right now, and I think about how you, Vega, are hanging in the balance—between life and death. It may be true that you are alive tonight, and it may happen that when I wake up in the morning, you will be dead.

Do you die when you are only 1.5 mm? Or maybe it's better to use the term "perish?" I dream of being able to save you, and I imagine what it would feel like to have a baby as small as 1.5 mm. It's unbelievable this is going to happen inside of me. It is my own body that will do this. Make the decision. Finish the selection. Maybe my womb will finish you off tonight. Or maybe you'll survive. Tonight. I pray for you. All while I know everything that happens was decided long ago. Because you are out there somewhere. You surround me and the cosmos surrounds you, we're gathered up in an impossible embrace. It's like having a snippet of heaven here with me, while I advance through some grey matter. All that will happen has already happened, and you, Vega, are out there among the stars.

07.07.2022

SUNDAY BLOODY SUNDAY

Googling can do strange things to a person. I usually stay off the internet for medical advice. But last night I was so worried and emptied of the power of acceptance that I gave in and kept searching and searching for info about bleeding during pregnancy. We discovered there was something called an implantation bleeding, which may occur when the embryo attaches itself to the uterine wall. We are in week four, so that fits perfectly. We were really fired up since this could almost be considered normal. The day started with another positive pregnancy test and a little more blood. This would be another day enveloped in ambiguity. We started out bravely, while the pain and blood gradually increased. We left for the beach, and I meditated on the mantra "All that will happen has already happened." It didn't work very well. When there was more blood again, something collapsed inside me and I heard myself say, loudly and coldly, "Ok, I get it."

Enough with the balance. The pain I was feeling was actually pretty intense, and I was actually bleeding quite a bit. That's it. I said it. A bloody day has come to an end, and I've calmed down a little bit. My body and soul are flat, out of charge, but there is more peace now. Something to react to. Something to withstand. It is easier to carry something—than to balance on the sharp edge of may-be.

I feel a kernel of worry. Is there an obstacle making things difficult? Will you ever find your way?

I study the vague lines of light in the ceiling from my bed. They are so beautiful. You are out there, but further away than I thought. I perceive a warm, dark being standing face to face with me. They have a shape that goes beyond all time and space.

This is the last evening of our travels. I came as one person and leave as a different one.

I came with you. I leave without you. I am not carrying anyone. I have no secret. Somewhere along the way, you fell off. The clock struck twelve and Cinderella has returned to her usual self. The glow is gone, and there she is, left in a gray world devoid of meaning and direction. I close my eyes and stare into the darkness behind my eyelids. There, the cosmos manifests itself, and I feel you so strongly, just a few light-years from me. Clear as a star, only larger and more diffuse. The beams extend to touch me, and there is something that feels as if my arms stretch toward you. They reach you, almost. There is a soft, golden light radiating from you, and you are.

08.07.2022

GENESIS

I wanted a last swim in the sea before we took off for the airport. I wanted to let myself sink into the ocean one last time. I submerged my head right away. No time to waste. Then I ran to rinse off in the refreshing outdoor shower by the simple change-rooms. The cool water ran pleasantly down my body. It was good to have something to carry, even if just a sorrow. I felt stronger now. I went in to change, tore off my swimming trunks. And inside there was something I'd never seen before. A dark, red lump with a white membrane. I knew immediately what it was. I knew what could have become you, was only 1.5 mm — and it was hidden inside this 1-2 cm lump. Was the white stuff the mucosa we had measured so many times during the ultrasounds?

Is this what it looked like? Or was this something else that had been growing around a four-week-old embryo? I felt afraid. As if I'd been surprised by a spider or some other creepy crawly. I left it there in my swimming trunk while I changed. I gazed at it several times, as if to check it was still there, slowly gaining control of myself. I wanted to befriend what was. But what was, was painful and a little disgusting. Inside me, there were emotions and sudden impulses running in every direction, but I dressed myself calmly.

I picked up my stuff and the swimsuit with the clump and went for the outdoor shower. I rinsed off the swimsuit and saw the mass fall down onto the pebbles and sand. I was immediately struck by bad conscience. I should have been more careful putting it down.

An old man came up to me—he wanted to shower. I attempted to kick the clump away to keep it hidden. I wanted to bury it a little with my toe. But I couldn't manage, and the man wanted his shower. Horrified, I walked to our car and started sobbing out loud when I sat down next to her. I told her what happened and knew I had to go back. I couldn't just leave it there. People would come there to shower all day. And between their legs the clump would be shuffled around in the water and sand, be stepped on. I knew it wasn't you, but you couldn't lie there. I wiped my tears and went straight back. I could see the clump right away, and I scooped it up with the sand it was resting in, so I wouldn't have to touch it. I came back to the car with a small pile in my hands, that I carried near my chest. "Put it down by the flowers," she said calmly. There were some white and red flowers there, and I dug a little hole by their roots. Nobody would step on it here. I knew that in time, small animals would find it, but that is part of the cycle of life.

Was it a grave, this hole I dug? I put the clump into the hole and covered it.

"Earth to earth. Ashes to Ashes. Dust to dust. And from dust you shall be resurrected," I heard myself say as I wept. There was a wilted flower there. I placed it on top. The peculiar little grave needed one more flower. I picked a lavender stalk and left it on top of the other flower.

TRUTH AND SEMANTICS

It's called a miscarriage, she said, in the middle of one of our many talks about the bleeding and you. We were in the car, in splendid summer weather, on our way down south on the E18. The flight back to a Norwegian climate and holiday mood hadn't made what happened in Crete as dreamlike and distant as I hoped. I could see the summer was lovely and warm, but I didn't really see it. I felt numb, as if there was a thin, grey film on my eyes. I turned quiet. "You're not on your period, you're having a miscarriage," she clarified. I had consistently labelled this bleeding as having my period. Fashioning it as a miscarriage was something else altogether. Having your period was a boring, trivial matter. A miscarriage was something serious and irrevocable.

10.07.2022

EXISTENTIALISM 2.0

Today, every trip to the toilet is a memorial service. After what happened on the beach in Chania, I have been bleeding continually. Not just blood, but something more substantial. I think, *there goes another fragment of what could have become you.* There, in the toilet bowl, a glimpse of what could have become a complete human life. And all I can do is flush it down. Was it now? Was that you? Was it nothing? Is it dead? Am I about to go off my rails? Another swim in the sea, this time in Kragerø, and yet another alien body in my swimsuit. The consistence is more solid this time. Maybe this was that 1.5 mm small creature we'd seen pictures of on the Internet. All I wanted, was to throw it out the window, but I could not do it. I had a tiny burial there in the heath by the summer lodge we slept in. How many burial grounds would we have in the end?

SILENTLY SWIMMING WILD DUCKS

I am daydreaming. From the dock by the cottage, I follow two birds on the fjord. One large, one small. A mother and a child. The usual thoughts come knocking, and always with a side of self-loathing. "Imagine, even two ducks make me think of children." I see how they belong together. The small one so tiny it disappears from my view behind each wave. The large one swims at a steady pace, and ducks into the water from time to time. That leaves the tiny one all alone on the surface. It looks lonely. And then the large one is back, and balance is restored.

There's a tightening in my uterus. I have to swallow a yelp. Hold it back. Pull my legs together while the pain pulls and twitches. Then it quiets down and lets off. That's what it's been like for the past day. No pain, and then a sudden strong tug that forces me to steady myself on something or pull my legs up. A few seconds with my jaw clenched, and then it is over. I am glad I have these contractions or whatever they're called. When I talked on the phone with the clinic two days ago, they told me to take a new pregnancy test in a few days, to make sure there was nothing left.

If it were positive, that would suggest not all had been expelled.

She didn't say anything more than that. And I wondered what would need to happen to me if all hadn't come out. I imagine things inside myself, and then react to it firmly and say to myself "I won't do that, I cannot go through that." For that reason, I welcome these fits, and I think my body is doing a thorough job of removing what no longer has any place there.

1 + 1 = 3

Scenes from the past few days are being replayed in my head, and I wonder what it is that I have buried. Maybe it wasn't anything "special." Imagine, standing there on a beach burying a bit of your period? I toy with the idea of standing there, during any cycle at all, crying about some menstrual blood in my hands and then burying it. And maybe there is some wisdom to this bizarre image. Maybe I haven't grasped the extension of what it means to appreciate all that is life. I think about how things are transformed from being one thing to being another. Menstruation, endometrial lining, follicles, all these things that exist in great quantities. We resist them. We take pain killers, we use pads, tampons, menstrual cups—and curse it all. The very same matter may in one moment be on its way to create a human, just to become waste in the next.

And what about sperm? A product of all that is masculine, lust-driven, a necessary evil in a boy's room, on the can. Phallus. Manhood.

Mars. And all these things the female body is able to do, the mystique and honour bestowed upon the female body. It is nothing without the other element. The man. It is only together, where both parties stop being one and gives up itself for the other, that life can come into—being.

And for the first time in I life, I have conciliatory thoughts about being a woman, and only being able to create life together with a man. Something inside me hurts when I write this. Even if we've been trying to have a child for exactly one year now, and I've wanted one for fifteen, I have—without effort—suppressed all this until now.

What was I so afraid of? I am shaped by the current cultural, sociopolitical narratives about women and men. It's part of my cultural DNA to be suspicious of men. But the man and the woman are not the culprits here, even if that is hard to believe. Neither one of them is more guilty nor more innocent. The Man and the Woman are manifestations of the primal duality of life, wherein all the big questions and motifs are embedded. Why were they created man and woman? Why not just create a human species with a single biological sex? But it is what it is: For life to emerge, two extremes need to meet and give up their origin.

The Man and the Woman have become symbols of all kinds of things. Notions, traumas, discrimination, and endless narratives about power — inequalities, abuse, and assault. Male chauvinism and feminism, a ramification of ideologies, thought patterns, political views, discussions, systems, polarization, pain, and hate. And deep down, when you see a human for what they really are, the Man and the Woman are as innocent as they were when they were newborn.

And I could see that I could love myself as a woman—and love men as men, and I desired to be a fertilized woman. It is much easier to hate than to fear. When we've reached our threshold of fear, we start hating. I have been too fearful, too hateful to allow myself these thoughts. And right after, other fear-driven thoughts return: "What about my partner? What's her role in this?" As if one would exclude the other. This is how they start, these short circuits that make our society combustible and riddled with conflict.

We are two women, two women who want to have a child together. In our age, we've come to expect to be able to have everything we want. Even if this is biologically impossible. The society we're a part of has developed solutions for almost every need. But we became vulnerable in our inability to take to heart the full scope—the true nature—of these solutions. I wanted a child with my partner, all while despising the men who sold their sperm to the sperm bank. I thought it would be possible to get pregnant all while I shied away from the idea of being impregnated. I've thought women can have babies without men. I didn't want to admit I only possess half of what is needed. I've been trained so well in this self-assured thinking pattern, which is based in a reluctance to accept things as they are. It is a biological truth that I have to be fertilized by a man, and the fact that this is possible, is a beautiful thing.

I want this now. I can move on.

I feel stupid and smug that I thought I could have a little child. That I could have it without bringing the necessary respect and humility for the other half that makes this possible. How could I isolate myself and only cast a half-glance on the homepage that shows all the donors? How could I scoff at their profiles, while at the same time clicking to check their shoe size or eye colour? How can I be filled by an unexpressed contempt for something I am part of myself? There's self-loathing of course, feeling ashamed that I don't have all that it takes, and having to resort to this. But this isn't something I resort to. I am not a victim. The only thing I've been a victim of, is myself.

And how would it be for you, Vega? If you came into a world that didn't acknowledge your origins. What would it be like to live with a mother who withheld some of the information about how you came into being?

There is a man out there. I don't know who he is. And he's given up something of himself for this. It's easy to be suspicious of his motives, or to minimize his contribution. But when it comes to it, his contribution is inestimable, and it will have effects on you until the day you die. I am grateful I've found the courage to admit this now, relieved that I am willing to acknowledge all parts of your origin. And I am sorry I have been part of a culture that produces irreconcilable differences between men and women.

23.07.2022

LOVE OR PSYCHOSIS?

I'm in the backseat of the car, on the way back from a concert. I look out across a fjord in Western Norway. The landscape slides past and I feel a slight tug in my belly. I felt it yesterday too. Tiny hints that something is about to happen. Another period. It's only been two weeks since I buried you in Crete.

We have agreed with the clinic that I should get in touch with them on the first day of my cycle. I am afraid it's too early for my body to accommodate you now. I look out the window and my thoughts circle around you. Episodes and glimpses from the past few months come back to me—and I remember them full of wonder. All the extreme thoughts—the self-loathing and shame especially. They seem so foreign to me now. As if they were products of a psychosis. I am uncomfortable when I think back on it. As if I could never be as heart-broken, then hopeful, then desirous—and then obsessed—again.

23.08.2022

TO WAIT—HESITANTLY

I'm on the train and watch the fields glowing with gold in the morning sun. A flock of birds lifts off from the ground—and I think of you.

Every day. Each time I see a child. Each time I dream of the future. I still have plans, inspiration and ideas—but they appear pale to me as long as you aren't there. I know, I know, you've heard all this before.

The first day of my cycle has arisen, and now the clinic thinks we need to add extra fuel, so-called supportive treatment. So now they have put me on Prednisone. I've taken that medication once before, when I had a really bad cold and needed to get my voice back before a concert. Why would they have me take it to get pregnant? It's a strong anti-inflammatory drug and the adverse effects, if you're on it for a long time, are not great. I showed up for the usual ultrasound, and my attitude was hesitant. I didn't want to start the emotional roller-coaster before absolutely necessary. During the ultrasound, the doctors pointed to a tiny black dot on the screen. A collapsed follicle. Meaning, the ovulation had already happened, and this cycle was already gone. I tried to achieve a balance between not feeling too sad and not becoming indifferent. I think I managed that. Part of me felt relief, because my body has felt unfamiliar since I buried you in Crete.

Murmuring aches come and go, I feel out of synch, off. My body needs time to become itself again. So, I look out the train window this morning in August, waiting—hesitantly.

ESCAPE ACT

People are so kind at the Voss hospital. The doctor was a relatively young woman, speaking a beautiful, polished Voss dialect. Fate had led me to the gynecological polyclinic at Voss since it had been revealed the ultrasound I did earlier in the week had happened too early in my cycle.

The follicle wasn't large enough, and the endometrium wasn't thick enough. I was in the same old doctor's office in Oslo when the doctor told me "So you'll have to come back here on Thursday," as a matter of course. That was on Tuesday morning, and I had flown from Bergen just to make it to that appointment.

I was supposed to be at work and had been dreading for a long while to tell them I couldn't come. I presented them with a version of reality that same morning through text and told them I had some meetings in Oslo. But who does that, travels to Oslo with no pre-warning? It is upsetting to present myself as something different than what I am. I have already lied to them several times at the strangest moments. Once it became clear I had to do an ultrasound when the summer concert with my students was scheduled, something I am often deeply involved in. I tried to dodge the truth as well as I could, but it was difficult to not just tell them the facts. But the longer I stay in this process, the more convinced I become I can only share with those who strictly need to know. This is why I have to become a different version of Josefin. Someone who doesn't always show up. It comes at a price.

When I returned to the doctor's office in Oslo, I was emptied of that energy that allows risky logistics. Six months ago, I had started planning how to get myself from a school trip at Voss to a gynecological exam in Oslo and back, in the shortest possible time. Preferably without anyone noticing. Now I just started crying and burst out, "it's impossible to plan anything at all!" The doctor understood. A woman's cycle doesn't bend to logistics or to my self-image as a dependable person. I cried as I explained my situation. She told me I could just as easily go to a gynecologist in Bergen.

I only had to pay for this myself. In my mind I imagined the drive to Bergen and back, and the lies I would have to present to my colleagues. I couldn't take that either. I went into detail—told her I was supposed to be on a cabin trip with my students... at Voss. I was already dreading the doctor's resigned reaction. Instead, she sounded cheerful. "Voss? But they have a great hospital there, and they are so easy to deal with. Actually, that is easier than Bergen. I'll just call them so you can have your appointment there."

I was at the breakfast table with colleagues and students, pretending like nothing was happening. At 08:55 I left the table and started running as soon as I had passed the corner of the hostel cabin. I launched myself into the car and drove as fast as I could through the center of Voss. And then I was there. The clock on the wall in the waiting room at the gynecological polyclinic at Voss showed 09:02. I was called in by the young, convincing-looking doctor. At 09:15 I was in a chair, watching a monitor with the black and grey shadows of my uterus. She wrote down the measurements on a report she would transmit to the clinic. I thanked her for the appointment, threw myself into the car and was back at breakfast by 9:30. On my way back, I had called the clinic and read the report from the doctor and attempted to avoid any misunderstanding. "Can you repeat that? Was it the right follicle that was 19X14 mm?"

DO YOU BELIEVE IN ME?

It is evening. I have been out in the woods to pee, and I prayed a prayer to you. Tomorrow is the day they will thaw you and transfer you back into me. Strictly speaking, you haven't been there before, but the part of me that is my egg comes from there. If I am to be completely honest, I didn't really pray to you. I thought about you and assumed you'd probably think it wasn't a good fit for you inside me. I feel shame that I do too many things. This means I don't take time off for you, and then you won't come. It's a strange pattern of thought I'm constructing. I am busy with so many things, travel here and there, to do talks, teach and play concerts. And if you come to me and discover I haven't calmed down of my own free will before you arrive, I will never be able to do it after you've appeared. That's why you choose to turn around. You don't believe in me. And slowly, I lose faith in myself.

DREAMCATCHER

It's been five days since you were transferred, and it's possible you already died. Maybe you died on Saturday, or yesterday. Last night I had a dream that I was in a doctor's office and two women doctors told me, "You need to start on a new treatment." When I asked why, they replied casually, "oh, yeah, it didn't work this time either. You aren't pregnant." Completely offhandedly and in passing. I tried not to dwell too much on it. That same morning, I received a message from her, which said "I dreamt we had a boy whose name was Vinde Mathias Winther…"

So, in the world of dreams, it was 1 to 1, and for the first time I felt real joy that you may be a boy. It's a strange thing to imagine. How my woman's body is also able to make a boy's body.

22.09.2022

THICKER THAN WATER

"If you cut yourself, you'll bleed more than normal," the pharmacist tells me without being asked. I had to ask her to repeat it, because I had no idea what she was referring to. While she reiterated, I understood this was about the stack of blood-thinning syringes between us on the counter. I would jab these into my belly for the foreseeable future. "You need to make sure you don't inject them at the same spot because that may cause lumps of fatty tissue that are hard to penetrate." Now I have bruises on my tummy and wonder what I will look like in a week. The injections give me a weird feeling in my stomach. It's like having muscle cramps, as if there are small animals in there crawling around. My body takes it in stride. My sleep quality worsens. I need to pee two to three times per night, and my digestion slows down. But beyond that, my body doesn't seem much affected by having three different medications it never asked for, administered every day.

STAY IN MY GARDEN AS LONG AS YOU WISH

I was roaming around in the forest and suddenly felt the urge to climb up a tree. I wanted to feel what it was like up there, where the wind rustles. It felt good, I thought about you, and wondered how it felt for you. Did you too experience that the connection I have to nature is also yours? Afterwards, I sat outside our house by an open fire. A daddy-long-legs came walking across the table. I was startled when it came towards me—embarrassed by my reaction. I was glad I was alone. Earlier in the day, I had tried to follow a daddy-long-legs on the forest floor but had to give up. It felt as if it knew I was studying it. Each time I was close enough, it stopped and just stood there. Can I do penance for all the hours I subjected my body to stress? Can you see that I'm doing all that I can, that there is hope for me?

26.09.2022

NOW OR NEVER

The adverse effects from all the medications are starting to bother me. It feels unnatural to inject myself every day with something that thins my blood. One shouldn't play around with such things, I think to myself. After injecting myself, my body is filled with a strange restlessness.

My muscles become like jelly and yet tense at the same time. My feet turn twitchy. Today I was unable to restrain myself, so I logged on to check the adverse effects of using blood thinners. The highlights were psychological conditions, bleeding, restlessness, bad sleep quality, death, moon face, weakened muscles and brittle bones. Tomorrow I may not need to take them anymore. Tomorrow I'll know if I'm pregnant. My thoughts are spiralling downwards. I now think I have nothing more to offer. If you don't arrive now, I'm simply not good enough. I will never get any better than this. Neither physically nor mentally. We'll have to put it to rest, I think.

27.09.2022

BRING IT ON

I couldn't make myself go to check the pregnancy test by myself. Three minutes had passed, and all I felt was heaviness. Ready for another slap in the face and things like that. "Come at me," I thought as she entered the bathroom to see. I stayed in the kitchen and followed her with my gaze. She turned towards me—and she smiled. We were happy. She was happier. I didn't dare to be happy. I didn't want to subject myself to all that.

WOMEN ON THE BRINK

"How much are you willing to sacrifice for this?" The question had seemed absurd a few months back, but now it had a different ring. Yesterday, I was in Sandefjord for a blood test. On my way there, I talked to a friend on the phone. She asked if I would consider requesting a sick note. She knew me and my tendency to push myself hard. She tried to get through to me with admonitions about how the body needs space and calm to be able to do this. With feigned serenity I told her how utterly unthinkable it would be for me to take sick leave. I knew she was right, but I didn't know how to break away from the way of living I had fashioned for myself. After fumbling around with words about how complicated it would be, I finally found the right argument to put the discussion to rest. "I've been doing this for a year and a half now, and if I had asked for a sick note for each attempt, I would have been on sick leave for about that long. So, I'm only trying to stay neutral, take things as they come." She bought it, and we could move on to something else. We talked about other matters while I was in the waiting room for my blood tests, but deep down I knew she was right.

In my car on my way home, I received an e-mail from a colleague. It caused me to throw my mobile on the floor. I was that angry. It was about something tiny and trivial, but I lost it. I noticed my reaction was unproportionate to say it mildly. When I came home, some other insignificant issue occurred, and this time I melted down. I called her and let it all flow out of me. I complained and sobbed. I couldn't do it anymore.

This is not doable. It's impossible to combine these things. The ultrasound at Voss, transfer in Oslo, blood tests in Sandefjord, a visit to the pharmacy in Tønsberg. And all of it in secret.

I couldn't take anymore. I cried and cursed. She took it all. Thank God, she took me in. Afterwards, I stacked wood while I finished crying.

I calmed myself and thought about how my friend on the phone had been closer to the truth than she herself understood. She pressured me, but in a humble manner, and my reaction after it was hard, but it released me. It felt good to finally admit this was all too much.

30.09.2023

OH, WHAT A MORNING

I was on the Bastø ferry that last morning of September. On my way to a concert in a women's prison, when I logged on the blood analysis app, "My Fürst."

A number appeared that felt like a billion: an hCG of 542. That is really high! Last time, we had 195, which seemed dizzying. Now I had reached about the same point, so a 542 had to mean my body was serious about this. I sat in the ferry lounge and looked out on the fjord. It was all grey, but to me it was glimmering. I let in a little more happiness.

WHO CHOOSES THE FALL?

The fact that you exist, enhances everything. The light in the world is brighter, but the darkness has also turned darker.

> The fall of Man is a choice
> Can that be true?
> The fall of Man is a choice
> Can that be true?
> But who are we if we are free
> And freely choose to fall
> From whom can we say we are free?
> And who chooses to fall?
> Fall. Fall.
> Man, fall.
> Man's choice.

BLACK THE NIGHT DESCENDS

I am on a path into darkness. I do all the things I'm "supposed" to. I write good songs, perform well at work, go for runs, do yoga, sleep every night. But darkness is descending on me, so slowly nobody is aware. So slowly, denial seems a reasonable reaction. I am sitting in the forest now. I have found a spot where all I can see is forest, wherever I turn. I run away into the woods, hoping the swish through the trees will force out the sound of my thoughts. My dirty, contemptible, repetitive, godforsaken thoughts. Sometimes the word "godforsaken" really resonates, and you allow the exaggeration because the word itself is so juicy. No, I am not exaggerating. These thoughts are forsaken by god. When I think these thoughts, I forsake god, and I assume god forsakes me?

I talked to my best friend over the phone to Iceland. I never call. I never call anyone. I never call anyone when there is a crisis, when I cry with loud sobs and feel fully alone. I never call when I should call—and talking to someone who loves me and knows would help. Today I called. I stuttered and talked incoherently about how everything had changed. It's as if my world has a new compass. That the compass is you.

A new, quiet force has entered. Some instinct that tells me I'd do anything to protect you. And if protecting means to not bear everything, then that's how things must be. Then I will stop trying to bear everything. If to protect you I have to give up who I thought I was, then I will give myself up. If that's what it takes to protect you, that's what I'll do. It's the same to me. Everything feels the same to me. My only purpose is to protect you.

How sweet. How classical. The mothering instinct, somehow. The lioness.

And every day I'm terrified you'll die. But now I'm past the point of pregnancy when I buried you in Crete. Now you've become even more real.

NOW I HAVE TO BEAR THAT I AM NO LONGER ABLE TO BEAR IT ALL

I went to your grave. We both know it isn't your grave. Living beings cannot have graves, and right now you are alive. But I am back in Crete—again. When we went to the beach, I had to go to the place where I buried what may have become you. I wanted to see what it looked like now. There was a strange flower there with a tiny stem and white, downy petals. And there was toilet paper lying around. It's clearly a place for people who don't want to use the rustic lavatories. Down in the sand lies something that could have become you, but which now has a different form. Maybe you've been eaten by tiny creatures, or flushed away by the rain, or maybe something in you nourished that puny flower. Whatever the case, you are not there. You are alive inside me. We have now entered the sixth week, and I thank god for every day that passes without any blood on the toilet paper. How strange it is to be here! I am pregnant for the second time in my life, and both times I've been on Crete.

Tonight, I've been reading research articles about the effect of prenatal exposure to cortisol. That is, what happens to you if I'm stressed out during this pregnancy. Despite my latent fear, I was surprised by how explicit and extensive the research was. To an extent you are protected from the cortisol I excrete, but not fully. The effect can be detected during your first year. You may show signs of higher activation, meaning you're more sensitive to stress—and have lowered cognitive functioning. It was about how I envisioned it, and as explicit as this quote, "Exposure to elevated concentrations of cortisol early in gestation was associated with a slower rate of development over the first postnatal year and lower scores on the mental development index of the Bayley Scales of Infant Development (BSID) at 12 months." Another one said, "Prenatal exposure to elevated maternal cortisol has been shown to predict increased fussiness, negative behavior and fearfulness in infancy."

I have to find some way to shield you—now—even if it's practically impossible to reverse how I've become sensitized in such a brief time. They call it the Neurosequential Model, and it goes like this: The more stress you experience, the more you're exposed to the effects of this stress. It's what we call a downward spiral. It's physiological, and I cannot override it just like that. But I can prepare for less stress.

I think of other women who have been pregnant, women who have lived through extreme situations, been poor, been victims of rape, threats, abuse, who have lived through war. I try to think, "Those women must have felt much more stress than me. What I feel is mere stress, I have no other trouble nor pain." But then I feel my whole upper body hiss, even when I'm in bed and have just meditated. It is my own fault. I have brought this on myself over time. I have born. I have thought one needs to bear.

And what does it mean to bear? Isn't it to expose yourself to something you can't, don't want or shouldn't? And which consequences arise from bearing? Pain is suppressed and takes on a different form. It doesn't disappear. There's a price to pay, some other time, some other place, in some other form. And now is the time to pay that price. Now I cannot suppress it anymore because you are the one paying. I've been so good at the only thing I cannot do. Now is my time to bear that I am no longer able to bear it all.

In two days, I will know if you're actually alive, if you're viable, that you're not floating around outside my womb or have come up with some other strange idea. That will be my first ultrasound that has potential to be really uplifting. That's when we have to start walking together, Vega. You have to help me in any way you can. And suddenly I realize I've written a song about this:

At long last, I don't know a thing
Imagine the day to be
At long last they clipped my wing
Now I'm here in my naked skin
All those who waited for so long
Wondered if it'd ever come
The day was better than we thought
The day turned smoothly on the dot
No more hiding places left
Who's a friend to the bereft?
Not one shortcut to be found
Our time has finally come around
Now learn the art of wanting nothing
Now learn the art of being nothing
Now learn the art of mastering nothing
Now learn the art of leaving things be
At long last, I don't know a thing
Imagine, I gave away my wing
At long last!

18.10.2022

PAIR OF HEARTS

Inside me, there are two hearts. One beats faster than the other. Your heart, Vega, beats faster than mine. I could see it. I could hear it. I heard the heartbeats, noticed the rhythm was even. I saw a tiny, bean-shaped shadow with a black dot, moving around pulsating. Today, you are seven weeks and two days old. On our way home from the ultrasound,

I decided to start afresh. Instead of going to the gym, I went to a yoga class. There they told us to imagine something we carried around that we could let go of. We could imagine it running off our shoulders as we lay in child's pose. I imagined all those negative thoughts, the fear, shame and self-loathing. I let it run off my shoulders and into my yoga mat.

03.12.2022

ONE MOMENT

"Now you can really tell!" she exclaimed, admiration beaming from her eyes. I could tell she found me beautiful. She tells me all the time. I have gained five kilos in the past three months. As far as I can tell, it's five kilos of pure fat. At least it feels like it. I don't give it much weight. The vanity in me notices my upper arms have become round and there is cellulite on my thighs. But most parts of me aren't affected. She just continued to look at me, tried to convince me I was beautiful. I looked down on my belly, which just looked fat—and dotted with faint bruises from all the injections I jabbed there. I negotiated with myself, landed on meeting her half-way. I chose to believe there is something beautiful about me—even now. I smiled back at her to show I accepted her compliment.

WAITING TIME

It's Advent. The time of the year Mary walked through thorny thicket, waiting for her child to arrive. During my life, I have sung so many songs about her waiting. Now I would write my own.

Hope — could it be true?
Doubt — will you carry me through?
Dream — was it you I witnessed?
Force — when I needed it best.
Want — what will it be like?
Comfort — the sorrow you'll strike.
Light — will you follow me?
Wait — the days I will see.
Time — turning winter to spring.
Prayer — I give my everything.
Scream — to you I will cling.
All is flux, all is transformation.
You—I give myself to you.
We —walk together anew.
Thanks — for all I will lose.
Night holding the shadows.
Of heaven's ocean meadows
Down — are you on your way?
To the vast, earthly play
What did you leave there?
Can you make us share in a joint yay?

DON'T CUT DOWN ALL THE WILDFLOWERS

In week twelve we had the special ultrasound for women over 35. We were told by the doctor that we were the least prepared couple they had ever had there. She asked for our health card, and I picked the blue health card you bring on vacation to the EU. She asked what our ideas were around the NIPT test, and we had no idea what she was referring to. She asked for blood tests from my family doctor and appointments with our midwife, but I didn't have any of that. I assume she was thinking that people who resort to IVF to have children, are so desperate they keep all their stuff in order.

The IVF pregnant person sits in the front row of her class, nodding eagerly to her teachers. I left the appointment feeling uneasy. Especially the question about the NIPT—noninvasive prenatal *test—and how that had been put to us.* The subtext seemed to be that this is something we were expected to make a decision on, that it was the normal routine to want to know if the baby had Down's syndrome. To me the idea felt foreign. What would I do with such information? It would not change anything for me. On our way into the hospital, we had passed two parents. Between them, a beautiful little girl with Down's syndrome, and as I admired her, I thought "we are about to make children like you extinct."

I've come to all my appointments since the midwife told me I wasn't well prepared. The bottom line is everything is in order, your heart rate is in order, your femur length is in order, my urine is fine, and you grow the way you're supposed to. I've met with the midwife at the local public health office and left there an hour later unsure what the purpose of that was, "Yes, I'm well. Yes, I weigh about 78 kg, yup, vegetarian, no, yes, it's correct—I neither smoke nor use snuff.

I sleep well, yes, and my digestion is fine. Yes, I take iron supplements. Ehm." During our conversation I started wondering what we were really doing, this stranger and I. Maybe they include such appointments to discover people who have great difficulties or who are unfit mothers. I started feeling self-conscious about the way I replied. I had been a little tired and sullen when our appointment started at 08:10. Maybe I should try to be more pleasant? Make a better impression or something. Bake some sweet buns if they came for a home visit. Then it turned out we're supposed to meet once a month first, and then once every two weeks.

09.01.2023

WE PREGNANT PEOPLE

I have obtained membership in a club. I have been admitted to a world only we pregnant people have access to. The news about you is out, and I'm beginning to sense how many times I will be told about how other women felt when they were pregnant, how little they slept the first part, how they felt when they found out they were to become a mother, what cravings they had, how bad the nausea was, before the concluding sentence, "you'll find your own way through." I've been included in some kind of women's community, where almost everyone I meet has lots of experience bubbling up to the surface once they learn that I've become a member.

A good friend of mine asked if I could send a picture. I didn't understand what she referred to. Then it occurred to me she meant a photo of my belly. I had to admit to her I didn't have one. I realized many people take photos of themselves as their bellies grow. It was the furthest thing from my mind that I should take pictures of myself where I show off my belly. Why would I do that? At the hospital we were given fliers with info about how to order 3D pictures of you inside my belly. The promotional pictures looked scary, as if the baby was made of clay or stuffed somehow.

I feel my best when you and I are in a state of flow. When we don't talk so much about it, when there aren't so many measurements, worries, opinions and congratulations. When we just relax and do ordinary things. When you grow inside me and taste samples of how lovely it is to be alive.

When I have a bite of a mango, laugh a good belly-laugh, or feel the sun on my face. No photos, no tests, and no opinions. You do your part, I do mine. And once and again I can feel your small arms and legs against the inside of my belly. And life is vibrant.

10.01.2023

VEGA

In the windowsill in the bathroom, there is a tiny silver box. The lid is bejeweled, and the inside is covered in velvet. There, inside, there's a tiny, heart-shaped note. On the note, the word, Vega, is written. She gave me this box long before you existed and long before I buried you. I cannot remember why your name is Vega, but that's always who you were. Today, the doctor was able to confirm that it's you who is on your way, that you are a girl, that you are—Vega.

AQUARIUM

I'm lying on the couch, and I sense you. Your movements are quick. As if there's a fish swimming around in my tummy. She wants to feel it, and I try to explain the movements are too tiny and too quick. I read about how you practice your breathing. You don't breathe in air. You are like a fish. If I had been in the same water with you, I would have drowned. But you're living well there.

You can breathe in water. You know you are becoming a person, so you practice pulling water into your lungs, so you know how to pull in air once you are out. That's when you will perform the great transition.

You'll breathe in air for the first time. A primordial gasp. The very first inhalation. All the way at one end of life—and imagine—one day you will also exhale one last time. All the way at the other end.

23.01.2023

TEN KILOS HEAVIER, ONE TONNE LIGHTER

21 weeks pregnant, and I feel like a butterfly. I'm alert, happy and strong. Not ripped, but strong in a deeper sense. I have my body, my health, my job and my girlfriend—and at the same time I have you. All at the same time. The feeling is huge. And yes, it feels like a super-power.

THE TRUE NATURE OF THINGS

Have you thought about where you want to give birth? What's your take on pre-natal classes? You should follow this blog about birthing! Did you sign up for pre-natal yoga? Just wait, things will get worse! I have some exercises you can do to prevent complications. Believe me, I've been through all that! No? Maybe it's a little too early. Think about it when you get closer to the date.

There's a subtle dissonance creeping into talks about you. It's noticeable how this theme is engaging to people, how many gain their most formative experiences through having children. They long to share that. I listen to them, see how their memories come alive at the back of their eyes. They disappear into their own reminiscing while they tell me how things will be for me. When they ask me what I think of something, there is a slight murmur inside. Whether I've decided where to give birth to you, if I want an epidural, if I want to give birth in a bathtub, if I've written my birth plan, if I intend to breastfeed you, where you'll be placed, where you will sleep, what kind of diapers you will use. I have no answers. I believe it appears as a kind of indifference or a happy naivety. But it is neither. I have never been more in touch with my own body, my own feminine… nature. I feel whole. My body changes day by day, my belly is big, my balance poor, my fitness level dwindling, I have less body strength, and the layer of fat on my arms and legs is growing.

There is chafing on the inside of my thighs. And all of this feels just right. You kick and move and keep at it. I have a hard time breathing after I've eaten dinner. It's hard to stand for a long time, hard to walk too far, painful to lie for too long. Everything is changed, and I feel as if it's always been like this. This is not something to form opinions about.

I do not need words or theories about this condition. My self and my body flow together and I sense that I'm who I was always meant to be.

Back in the conversation, I reply that I'm well, I'm happy. The response suggests this isn't good enough.

Pregnant people are seemingly supposed to have more to carry on about. They should opine about things.

But you don't need any opinions. You have everything that you need. We know all we need to know, without knowing anything at all.

18.03.2023

GAS BALLOON

In the beforetime, you were a gas balloon. You floated around up among the clouds, among the stars, and I held an invisible string down here. You had a name long before you were anything at all. You were—before you existed. Light as a feather and completely incomprehensible for anyone—but me. Now you are heavy and real for everyone. So heavy my back is aching. So heavy I've started taking the elevator. So heavy, I wobble when I walk.
23.04.2023

I WON'T CUT MY HAIR UNTIL MY KINGDOM IS UNIFIED

I'm working in my garden. My back feels stiff, and the belly is in the way every time I bend to pick up the leaves I'm raking. I love to work. She is away, but I'm not alone. There is somebody else here that I weave through conversations with. You are in there and get moved around, twisted and thrusted. And sometimes there's a tiny comment from you through a movement. There's two of us. We are dancing.

My thoughts flow so well while I am working. And now they go back to that time in my mid-twenties. I recall that I from time to time thought I should get sterilized. The idea occurred mostly when I suffered through period pain. I thought, what a waste of pain and blood, when I would never carry a child anyway. I should just get sterilized. It never came to any more than passing thoughts, occasionally, but it hurts to think about it now. It hurts to think I was once such a stranger to my own body.

Earlier today, I tried to "relax" and sat down to watch the first episode of "Health food Furuseth." It was too uncomfortable to watch, so I went out to rake leaves instead. Else is supposed to lose weight, and will enter this world of body, health and overweight in a progression of episodes. I couldn't handle watching another expression of how alienated we've become. The Norwegian Broadcasting Corporation takes a methodical approach to explain how people get fat. Not a word is spent on what in a deeper sense is the most crucial factor: our lack of unity between mind and body. The whole series is founded on the very sad—and wrong—premise that humans are one-dimensional machines. Reductionist explanations based on cause and effect, but nothing about connection—or our lack of connection.

It was likely the «itch» left by the program that made me think back to my 20s and my own alienated relationship with my body. I chuckle as I tidy up some logs that are to be cross-cut and chopped. A few days ago, I received an e-mail from an agent who had seen my profile on a modelling website. It is tempting to lie here, to say I never created such a profile. But I have to admit I did, once, a few years back. I thought it would help my music career if I were visible on other arenas as well. But I quickly lost interest and forgot about it, I had to laugh when I saw the email from the agent.

Imagine if he'd seen me now—the contrast from this to the images on the internet. I started a project similar to that of Harald Fairhair the day I started waiting for you, and decided I wouldn't cut my hair before you were born.

That was nearly three years and 40 cm ago. The long hair on top of a 90 kg body, carried around by what soon may be defined as cankles. I wobble around wearing the same unshapely outfits every day, and I've started in advance to take advantage of the fact that parents of young children don't make a big deal of stains on their clothes. The gap between my self-image back when I apparently was able to create this profile, and how I feel now, provided comic relief. And I have never felt better.

It hurts to think that I once was sufficiently alienated to think about destroying my body. Destroying what now has become you. I think of all the people who live with the muted pain of believing you *have* a body, and from there start treating it like an object. And then they start identifying as this object. First you move the body out of itself, and then you follow that move yourself. In this kind of world, it makes sense to listen to explanations from an obesity expert about why we get fat. "You do this, and then your body does that." As if these are two different things, when what we need is to see we are one.

RELATIONSHIP STATUS: PREGNANT

It is peculiar to observe how a pregnancy changes the framework for how I'm perceived. If I by accident forget something, every time someone has answered, full of compassion, something along the lines of "Oh, right, are you noticing you've become more forgetful? It's common when you're pregnant. And then there'll be Mom Brain, so you'll have plenty of things to blame it on from now on!" If I tell somebody about some project I am doing at home, like redecorating, gardening or just tidying and cleaning, it elicits answers such as "Oh, you're building a nest, you're nesting."

It leaves a slight sensation of being stuck, as if I cannot be seen as anything but a pregnant person.

19.05.2023

THE PASSING OF GENERATIONS

Dear Vega. There are two divides in life. One is crossed when we are born, the other—when we die. These divides can only be passed once, and when that is done there's no way back. You cannot cross the divide backwards into unbornness. You cannot die and then cross the divide back into life.

Soon you will cross one of them, Vega. You are here now. We talk about you. You move, and we are able to see an elbow or a foot stick out, making my belly look really odd. You exist. When you are born and come to this world you cannot change your mind. There is only a single direction then, and it goes through life. You step into time and become subject to all the same forces as everyone else. Time becomes your ruler—and the forces of life, your matter. For the first few years, a timelessness will hang like a veil over your existence. But as time passes, the veil will be pulled aside, and you will wake up here, in our reality. Gravity, time, the weight of your body. All this will become your world.

And for a while you will forget there was another one, and you'll believe all this which pulls and subdues and lifts you there, is all that there is.

You may lose yourself to this world, you may become resigned. And you should too. For a while.

As life goes by and you get older, you will feel that shadowlike phenomena will play little tricks on you, behind a surface that felt as solid as concrete.

Your body is no longer being built up. It's starting to let itself go.

Go down and back to the earth. The time has come to be closer to the world—and what's earthly—in a new manner. You have to grip it and let go of it at the same time. It's a balancing exercise most never get around to.

But without it, aging may feel hard, and life is not fully expressed, and you live an illusion that you are your body. And then you start dying together with your body. When death approaches, it may frighten you, because it is you who will die. But you will not die. You will cross over the second divide in life, just like you once crossed the first one.

Soon you'll be born into a world you have no notion of, a world you only sense through sound, movement, light and spirit moods washing over you. And when you die, you will also be born into a world you have no notion of, but only sense through shadows, moods, light, and glimpses—from a world behind this world.

The divide you're about to cross, you will cross together with me.

To me too it will be an irreversible before and after. Carrying you inside me is beautiful and awe-inspiring, but when you have arrived, I will never again be who I used to be. I will forever be connected to you, to your choices, your sadness and joy, to your ascents and falls. You don't need to worry about me. You should follow your life's path. But you will have me, as an appendix filled with love and emotions, endlessly thinking of you, supporting you and feeling your troubles as if they were my own. Don't let me hamper you, not even when I impose with my compassion.

Just know, that's how things are, because a part of me will be born together with you. A part of me is you. I, too, am a part of someone. I know how much my mom thinks about me, how much she misses me and lives alongside me in my intricate life. When I leave her to go to a home in a different city, her heart aches. She hides it as well as she is able to, but sometimes, when I'm about to leave, she will hum "Every time you go away, you take a piece of me with you," completely unaware.

And then there will be a time where I will cross the second divide. Then I will have to leave you here, and you will be the eldest in your family. You will be the one to guide, who stands on the frontline and looks death in the eyes. That's when you have to face death head on, and spare someone else from being in that position. To be the head of the family also implies you will be the one to carry the relationship with death.

The one who will cross the divide first. You will not carry that just for yourself.

You will carry it for the whole family, you will be their shield. I will no longer exist as a body then. My scent, my hands, my gaze, my voice. They will all be gone. But I will be here as shadows in the wind, and you'll feel my presence even and anon. You will meet me in your dreams, you will hear my voice in your inner dialogues, you will stop for a moment while you are in the kitchen and feel a connection to someone who's not in the room. And you'll know it was me and be filled with a need to hold on, but as you grip at me, I will already be gone.

You will know that you shouldn't have, and you will believe I may have stayed longer if you hadn't tried to clench me. It's OK if you grieve me, and you should know that I long with all that I have, to embrace you and carry you just like I carry you now. But you may also close your eyes and listen to the hidden silence behind the sounds that surround you. Because it is there that you'll find me. You may listen to the wind through tree crowns and hear them sway. That will give you a glimpse of the weightlessness where I am. Where you were when I was here.

Sometime in the future, you will also cross the second divide. And I will not be there then. You will have to cross it alone. Everyone has to. If you lived connected to the most profound parts of yourself, you won't be afraid. You will sense that you're going to a place you know, and letting go of your clutch on the world holds many good things. The world's beauty, intensity, closeness and liveliness have been a weight you've carried and that wore you out. At this point you can put it down, and parts of you may become weightless again.

That's how you are now.

And just as tightly as we are woven into each other's arms, lost in each other's gaze, glued to each other's skin and in love with each other's smile when we lived here together, we'll be close in a new way when none of us is bound by earthly boundaries.

Because nothing ends. It only takes on a new form.

END OF PREGNANCY

"Did they walk you through the end of pregnancy procedures when you were here for your checkup?" the doctor inquired over the phone. I had to ask her to repeat the question, since I distinctly thought I heard her say "end of pregnancy," and imagined that must have been in error. I was at a café in front of an avocado toast and felt about the same as I had for the past month. She repeated it to me, reaching pregnancy week 42+0 implies the pregnancy is over. I was baffled at being told over the phone that my pregnancy was over, despite being completely pregnant and alive as I sat there. You too were alive—I could feel it.

It was an onerous conversation to have. I had decided beforehand I would not argue or try to convince her there were more sides to the issue she elected to present as one-sided. I would pretend to be slightly young and dumb, but without letting go of the idea that I wouldn't discuss inducing labour that day. She was more authoritarian than I expected, so pretending to be young and dumb became even more important. If I had started arguing, or showed her myself as I really am, I would have triggered her authoritarian side and provoked her to let out even more threats and admonitions. I knew I would have to process all the fear she launched in my direction. And that is no small feat when you are responsible for a child. There were several rounds of conversation, where each round started with her saying, "At this point, the fact is, it's better for your baby to be outside than inside your belly," and then pointed out the increased statistical risk that something could go wrong. And on my end, I replied with language such as "I would rather not" or "I would like to wait a little longer." In the end she decided I should call and tell them if I chose to come in later that day.

The rest of the day, the conversation reverberated in me. It was remarkable how fear pressed against all channels and seeped in. It was almost midnight when I headed out for a walk in the forest.

Several times during my walk I thought about a post I had seen on Facebook that day. The title was "Be Tick Smart." I read it by accident, even if I knew I shouldn't have. It laid out in detail how ticks were spreading—and all the connected dangers. I walk in the forest every day and spend lots of time in the garden, and I often have to get rid of a tick or two when the day is over. While I walked through the blue-grey twilight in the forest, it bothered me that these fear-inducing messages had reached through to me. The conversation with the doctor and the post about ticks had the same effect on me. It sowed fear in me about something that should be the most natural thing in the world. "Avoid walking on grass," was the message from one side. "Your pregnancy is over," was the message from the other. I thought of all those who are affected by this and stop walking on grass, or who go to the hospital to treat something that is an entirely healthy and natural condition.

20.06.2023

THE DAM BREAKS

The forest felt renewed. It had been granted a new spring. After several weeks of blistering sun in June, it was as if the rain had accumulated. Everything became too tight, too hot—and then it burst. And the rain came down. Finally. It rained copiously for two days, and at the same time you arrived.

I had walked around on dry paths waiting for you. The forest floor was dry as dust, and even green June-leaves on the tallest beech trees had started to look doubtful. What would happen if things continued like this?

Water was retained in my legs—it was too hot for somebody past their due date—and it was too hot for the forest. Bumble bees searched for water, and we were still waiting. Then the dam broke. Both the one in the skies, and the one which enveloped you.

21.06.2023

N I R V A N A

I have long imagined that you can reach a state called nirvana—or awakening—only through mental practice. I had learned that through improving my inner life, I would be able to become one with existence. I have hoped to reach it in this life, if nothing else, at least as small glimpses. I have thought of it as something out there, far in the future. And it was a surprise that I would experience it so undeniably. And it was a surprise it happened through giving birth. The pain was of a magnitude I didn't have language for. I growled and moaned, screamed and cried. The measured calm and deep breaths I had visualized I would display as I entered into it, were absent. I was angry, I was in despair, but I never felt panic. The expulsion phase lasted almost four hours, and I went back and forth between intense contractions and falling asleep, exhausted, between them. I slept deeply for one to two minutes at a time. Then I was woken up again when a contraction took hold of my body, and I roared. I roared from someplace inside me that I didn't know was there. The pain was too deep for me to think anything about it or about myself. I had to become one with it. The pain turned me to nothingness, it erased the idea of me.

I became nobody, and through that, I became everything.

23.06.2023

VOLUNTARY COERCION

"But can't we just place her in the windowsill and make sure she gets plenty of daylight?" we asked, when the jaundice level rose a little above what was recommended. The midwife wanted us to come back the next day to take a new test. "Oh no," she said with a chuckle, "that's what worked in the olden days." I was taken aback by this expression, and wanted to ask if she heard what she was saying. We were told again and again by the health services that we needed to shelter these first days with you on earth, that we needed to make room to just be together, the three of us, alone. At the same time, not a day had passed since you were born without them wanted to prod and assess you. We wanted to go home the same day but met resistance. The attending doctor had left for the day, and they had to examine you before you could leave.

We stayed overnight but were still told how leaving "so early" caused problems, that we needed to come back for more tests. "We never met anyone who declined," the nurse said when she suggested something called Newborn Screening. This was a test that is offered to detect a range of very rare diseases. We had just replied we didn't want Vega to be subjected to more tests than absolutely necessary. But many "offers" were in reality given with clear expectations attached—and warnings about the risk we exposed you to if we didn't take the offer.

Your vision, hearing, weight, hips, vitamin K-injection, reflexes, muscle tone, head circumference and oxygenation were some of the items that needed checking. We constantly tried to communicate that we wanted to protect you from too many stimuli during these first days, and we pointed out you had been examined by both the midwife and the pediatrician, and not least: you seemed completely healthy.

"It was really ballsy of you to withstand the pressure to induce the birth, I have to say. And going through such a hard birth without any anesthesia was impressive. We have fallen into the wrong ditch in this system," an experienced midwife said when we were about to leave. She brought her hand up to her mouth, looked ashamed and said, "now I have said too much." We were pleased with the praise, but the last gesture left us with a bad feeling.

On our way home from a bilirubin test and a hearing test, on our third day of assessments after birth, I received a call from an unknown number. I considered letting it ring. I already had one lost call and a text from the midwife at the public health station who wanted to come for a home visit. I had declined politely, suggesting we could make an appointment after the weekend. "Hello, it's Josefin," I said. "Hi, it's your daughter's public health nurse, I just wanted to hear how things are going. Have you started breastfeeding? Does she eat well? And how are you doing physically? I would like to come and visit you at home, and I am wondering what would be a good time for you." I felt baffled I was getting these questions over the phone by someone I'd never met. I told her I had already been contacted by her colleague, and asked if it was correct they both wanted to come on separate home visits. She replied that the child has a right to their own public health nurse. I sensed how strange it was to consider you as something different than me. You had lived inside me for forty-two weeks and three days, and only three days had passed since I gave birth to you. Now you'd become an individual in the eyes of the system, with your own rights, and clearly your own advocates. I explained we had already spent the past three days on different tests and that we wanted to protect you from more impressions and meetings right now. After once again using my tentative and gentle rhetoric, she agreed we could wait until after the weekend to make an appointment.

LET NOBODY IN HERE

I'm woken up by my own whimper. I dreamed. In my dream I'm standing on the stairs in front of our house. It's twilight. A figure crosses the lawn in front of me. It's wearing a hooded robe, it glares toward the house, but keeps walking straight forward. A kind of ghost. A living dead.

It wants to come into the house. More figures. They are blurred. They want to come in. They stand vigil outside. They don't wish us well. I stand on the stairs blocking the door in. I know who they want. They want you. But they need to get past me. I roar. They pull back, but slowly they start returning towards us. I roar, louder and louder. Nobody is allowed to touch you. Nobody! I roar in the way I've done only once in my life—when I gave birth to you. I'm awoken by my own yelps. You sleep right by me. I close the window. Nobody will be let in here.

ONE SKATE OR TWO SKATE STYLE?

"What breastfeeding technique do you use?" your public health nurse asked with a disapproving look. We were inside an office at the public health station after weighing you. You had lost 8 grams since you were weighed last time during the home visit earlier in the week, and you were not following the curve. We suggested we could be careful, weigh you at home and send her messages with the updates, but were told that wasn't enough. We had to come to the public health station. We were unsure if this was an offer or an obligation—we had been unsure about that in all our dealings with the health care system since the birth.

I felt like replying "I go back and forth between classical and skating style,", to push back against her master suppression techniques. But I chose, as usual, to subdue myself. I told her I didn't have any specific breastfeeding technique, while looking bewildered. By doing that, I felt I had failed some undefined test, and I left the place with a churning of shame and rage in my stomach. If she had meant to be helpful, it was a peculiarly condescending way to provide help. It took a long time to calm my mind after visiting the public health station, but fortunately I have been active in sports my whole life. When faced with resistance this way, it stirs my competitive instinct. I was filled with grit and "I'll show you-ness" and started a persistent pumping regime. That weekend I only did three things: I breastfed you, pumped and fed you the extra milk. We returned on Monday, and when the scale showed you had gained more than 300 grams, I really wanted to say something like "Now, what do you have to say? What breastfeeding technique do you think this was?" Instead, both of us knew the cool thing would be to look completely unruffled, so we just said, "That's nice. Was there anything else?" in a measured tone. When we left, with you between us, we probably glowed like two teens on their way from the last major test before the summer holiday. Tiny joys.

01.07.2023

P I E T À

We swim in each other's eyes. Images show up in me in glimpses. Glimpses of women. Women on a mountain farm 200 years ago. Women in war. Women in the Roman Empire. Virgin Mary. Slave women. Women wearing corsets. Women burned at the stake. Women in concentration camps. They all have newborns. They carry their tiny child, the newborn human. They shield and protect it against a brutal world. They have none of the things I have now. Nothing. Measuring instruments, baby bathtubs, bedding, baby oil, a roof over their head, quiet and safety. Several times a day I am sent into a current — racing through history. Especially when I look at you. I watch you and feel a heart-rending love and this deep tenderness because you are so completely vulnerable. Something bursts in me. Now I comprehend the endless interest in this motif through all our cultural history. Maybe the greatest motif of them all: the newborn child. Natality. The motif of our greatest holiday celebration, Christmas. A child and its mother's love. As if I dive into the river of history and become one with the hard work of women. I can see how women gave birth to the child and took care of it, while the outside world threatened from all sides, through every age. They carried their pain inside, in silence. Poverty, hard work, hunger, danger, they withstood all of this, so the defenseless child could live, grow up.

How did they know how to support the baby's neck? How did they know all these things we are told about nowadays? Mothers knew — and passed their wisdom down to their daughters. Sisters knew and passed their wisdom on to sisters. Women knew and passed the wisdom on to women. With its invisible thread, motherly love weaves the history of the world together into a tapestry.

03.07.2023

TELL ME, WHERE DID YOU COME FROM?

You sneeze. I wonder how you know how to do that. You look at me and a wide smile expands in your face. How do you know how to smile? We are in the middle of a song, something both of us enjoy greatly. We hum as we look deep into each other's eyes.

Suddenly there's a shade passing across your face, and you burst into tears. It is heartbreaking to look at. Where did that emotion come from? What did you hear? How do you know how to cry? What are your thoughts when you lie there and look at the window for what seems like forever? What do you see when you look at me?

In your gaze I feel completely naked and fully loved.

Tell me, where did you come from?
Tell me, where were you before?
Did you live far from this home?
Is that our after-shore?
Were you swept by the wind?
Up with the clouds, dinned?

Did you play among birds?
Then called away by words?
Tell me, who did you leave behind?
Tell me, who did you know there?
Were they loving-kind?
Did you feel the day draw near?
Were you in the ocean waves?
Playing with deep-sea braves?
Do you long to go back?
Or is this your chosen track
For waiting, crying, hoping, losing
Grieving, waking, winning, life-inducing
Tell me, where have you been?
Tell me, what were your thoughts?
Did day and night have their spots?
Was the sky blue to you?
Do you long to go back?
Or have you come to peace
Imagine, you wanted to come here!
Imagine, we're both here, you and me!

REFERENCES

Sangen om den røde rubin (untranslated, in English: The Song of the Red Ruby) – Agnar Mykle

Every time you go away – Paul Young

Svart senker natten seg – Arvid Rosén (untranslated, in English: Black Descends the Night)

The Timing of Prenatal Exposure to Maternal Cortisol and Psychosocial Stress is Associated with Human Infant Cognitive Development – Elysia Poggi Davis and Curt A. Sandman

To *err* is human, to forgive divine – Alexander Pope

Don't cut down all the wildflowers – Patti Smith

Å for en morgen – Jan Eggum (Untranslated, in English: Oh, What a Morning)

Slekters gang – B. S. Ingemann (Untranslated, in English: The passing of generations)

Sunday Bloody Sunday – U2

Pain is inevitable, suffering is a choice – Old buddhist saying

Raw youth – Margreth Olin

Vær i min hage så lenge du vil – Jarl Goli (untranslated, end English: Stay in my garden as long as you wish)